AF379424
EXTREME
SURVIVAL

space

Business Leaders

Engineering Wonders

Extreme Survival

Feats of Courage

Hacking for Good

Incredible Comebacks

Military Might

Sports Superstitions

Unusual Jobs

Women in Combat

Wrongly Accused

Photo credits: page 9: Kathy Hutchins/Shutterstock.com; page 16: Jeff Hutchens/Getty Images News via Getty Images; page 22: Lisa Maree Williams/Getty Images Entertainment via Getty Images; page 26: Matt Winkelmeyer/ Getty Images Entertainment via Getty Images; page 29: Claudio Villa/Getty Images Sport via Getty Images; page 30: Bill Ingalls/NASA/Getty Images News via Getty Images; page: 31: Songquan Deng/Shutterstock.com; page 33: Noel Vasquez/Getty Images Sport via Getty Images; page 34: MPI/Archive Photos via Getty Images; page 35: Getty Images/Hulton Archive via Getty Images; page 36: Scott Nelson/Getty Images News via Getty Images; page 37: Keystone/Hulton Archive via Getty Images; pages 46: Justin Sullivan/Getty Images News via Getty Images; pages 47: AMFPhotography/Shutterstock.com; pages 48/49: Paula Bronstein/Getty Images News via Getty Images; pages 50/51: Portland Press Herald/Portland Press Herald via Getty Images; page 53: U.S. Coast Guard/Getty Images News via Getty Images

ISBN: 978-1-68021-748-3
eBook: 978-1-64598-054-4

Printed in Malaysia

29 28 27 26 25   4 5 6 7 8

TABLE OF CONTENTS

CHAPTER 1
THE WILL TO LIVE

Frostbitten fingers dig into the cold ground. A woman crawls out of a wrecked plane. No one else is alive. Alone, she shivers in the snow. The woman pushes herself up. She takes one shaky step. It is her first step toward survival.

Anyone can end up in an unexpected situation. Hikers fall in the wilderness. Storms put people in danger. A boat sinks at sea. To survive these events, basic needs must be met. Survivors need enough air to breathe. Water and food are required to power the body. Shelter is needed for protection.

Meeting basic needs keeps the body alive. But survival is also mental. Staying positive is important. Many survivors think about loved ones. This keeps them going.

No matter what, survivors don't give up. They think through their problems. Focusing on small goals helps. **Resourcefulness** is key. Survivors push themselves. Only then can they make it out alive.

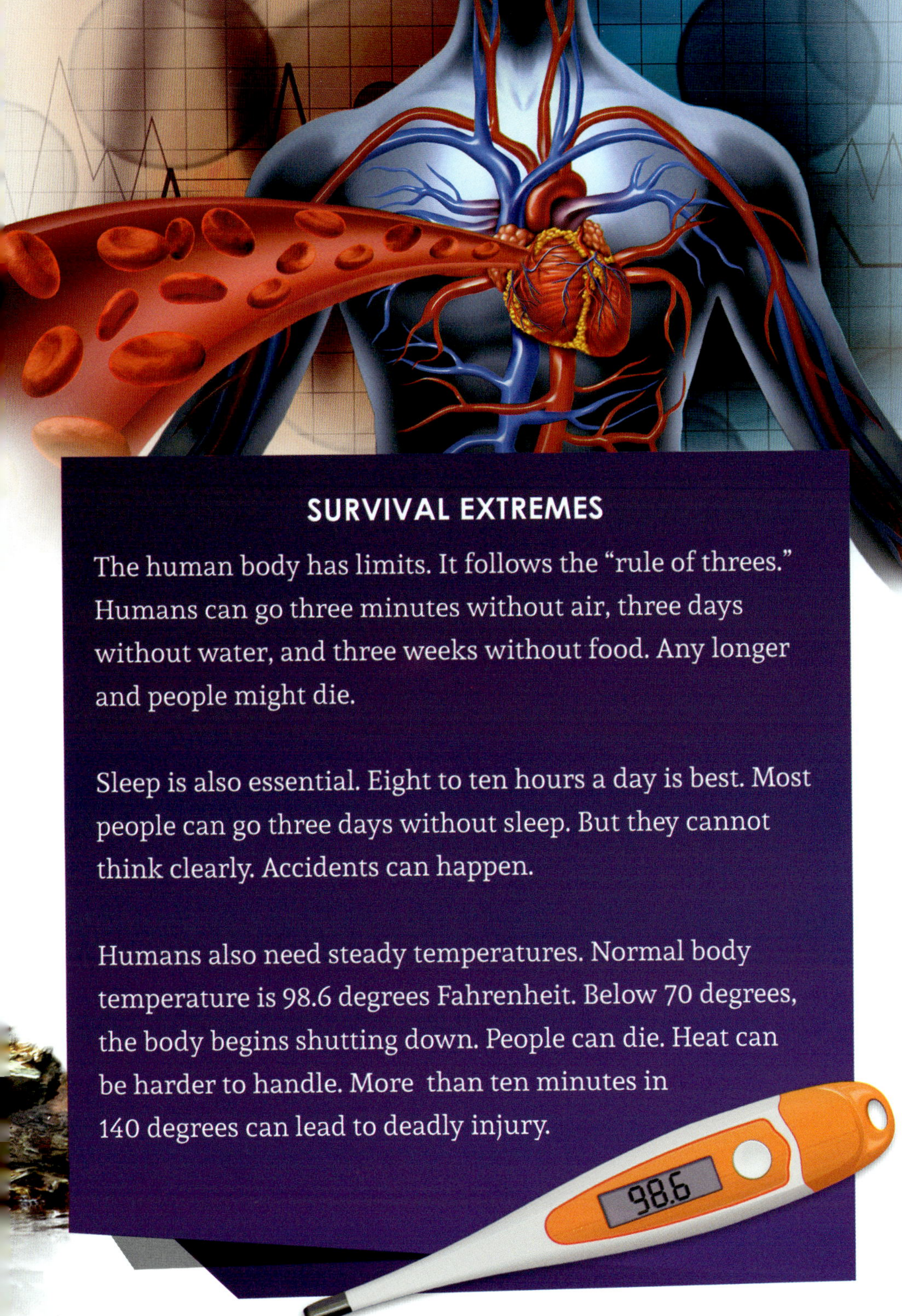

SURVIVAL EXTREMES

The human body has limits. It follows the "rule of threes." Humans can go three minutes without air, three days without water, and three weeks without food. Any longer and people might die.

Sleep is also essential. Eight to ten hours a day is best. Most people can go three days without sleep. But they cannot think clearly. Accidents can happen.

Humans also need steady temperatures. Normal body temperature is 98.6 degrees Fahrenheit. Below 70 degrees, the body begins shutting down. People can die. Heat can be harder to handle. More than ten minutes in 140 degrees can lead to deadly injury.

CHAPTER 2
THE SEA

Oceans cover 71 percent of the earth. People like to go boating and fishing in these salty waters. Others work on ships. Sometimes a trip goes wrong. Now these people must fight for their lives.

It was 1983. Tami Oldham Ashcraft and her fiancé, Richard Sharp, had a job. They were hired to take a boat from Tahiti to San Diego. This should have been an easy trip. Both were experienced sailors.

Three weeks in, a hurricane hit. Ashcraft was knocked unconscious in the storm. When she woke, her fiancé was gone. Alone, injured, and in shock, Ashcraft kept going. She rigged the broken boat as best she could. Using only her watch and a sextant, the sailor navigated the open sea. After 41 days, she made it to Hawaii. In 2018, Ashcraft's incredible story of survival was made into a movie titled *Adrift*.

TAMI OLDHAM ASHCRAFT

Amanda Thorns was a sailor. She was crossing the Atlantic Ocean in 2010. Her father and a friend were with her. There was a very bad storm. Waves swelled to 30 feet. Then something terrible happened. Ropes from the boat tangled around Thorns's father. He was swept into the sea and lost.

Thorns wanted to give up. Instead, she and her friend fought to survive. Eventually, the seas calmed. But the boat's engine and mast were broken. The two survivors made repairs. A new mast and sail were built. After 12 days, a ship rescued them.

In 2015, Louis Jordan went on a fishing trip. He sailed from South Carolina. During the night, stormy weather hit. The small boat flipped over. His family became worried. They reported him missing. The **Coast Guard** searched but could not find him.

Jordan's boat righted itself. He stayed inside to keep out of the sun. There was enough canned food for the first few weeks. After that, Jordan fished and drank rainwater. Two months later, a German ship found him. He was 200 miles from the North Carolina coast.

SURVIVING THE TITANIC

On April 10, 1912, the *Titanic* set sail. The ship left from England and was heading to New York. Four days later, it hit an iceberg. Land was 400 miles away. Less than three hours later, the ship sank.

Passengers were put on lifeboats. Most were women and children. Another ship picked them up. Those who couldn't fit on lifeboats were in the ocean. These people did not live long. The water was 28 degrees. Few people were saved from the water.

Less than 32 percent of people survived. In 2009, the last living survivor of the *Titanic* died. The woman was 97. When the *Titanic* sank, she was two months old. A lifeboat took her to safety.

DEADLY ACCIDENTS AT SEA

Le Joola (2002)

Off the Coast of Gambia/Atlantic Ocean
The passenger ferry sank in five minutes during a storm.
Deaths: About 1,800 | Survivors: 64

Tek Sing (1822)

South China Sea
The *Tek Sing*, called the "*Titanic* of the East," hit a reef and sank.
Deaths: About 1,600 | Survivors: 200

Halifax Explosion (1917)

Halifax, Canada
Two ships collided and caused a deadly explosion.
Deaths: About 2,000 | Injuries: 9,000

Doña Paz (1987)

Marinduque, Philippines
The passenger ferry hit an oil tanker in shark-infested waters.
Deaths: About 4,000 | Survivors: 26

CHAPTER 3
ANIMAL ATTACKS

Seeing wild animals can be exciting. But these creatures can also be **threatening**. They can be strong and fierce. Most are not used to humans. This can lead to danger.

In 2016, Todd Orr was up with the sun. The Montana hunter was hiking. Suddenly, a branch snapped. A grizzly bear was charging. Quickly, Orr used bear spray. But it did not stop the animal.

Orr threw himself on the ground. He wrapped his arms around his head and neck. The bear bit and scratched him before leaving. Soon after, the bear came back. This time was worse than before. Staying calm, the hunter played dead.

Finally, the bear left. Orr picked himself up and drove to the hospital. First, doctors closed his wounds. This took eight hours. He later had many more surgeries. Doctors repaired his torn muscles and skin. After months of physical therapy, Orr recovered.

Michael Fay is an explorer and a **biologist**. In 2002, he was in Gabon, Africa. Elephants can be dangerous, but Fay was not afraid. He was used to the animals.

One day, Fay came across a mother elephant. She began to charge. As Fay ran away, he tripped. The animal tried to **gore** him. Fay grabbed her tusks. He moved his body out of the way. The elephant pressed him into the ground. It broke his ribs.

Then the elephant tossed him, and he hit the ground. When Fay opened his eyes, the animal was gone. His arms and back were wounded. But he had survived.

16

HOW TO SURVIVE AN ANIMAL ATTACK

It is best to stay away from wild animals or watch them from a safe distance.

If a bear comes close, do not run. Move slowly. Make a lot of noise. This can scare the bear away. If the bear attacks, play dead. Lie facedown and protect your head and neck with your hands.

Do not run from a cougar either. Shout and wave your arms. Throw rocks. If the animal attacks, aim for its eyes.

Snakes in the wild can bite. Treat all snakebites seriously. Call 911. Apply pressure to the bite. Stay calm. Do not move. Take a picture of the snake, or write down what it looks like. This can help doctors figure out what type of snake it is. Then they can use the right medicine.

CHAPTER 4
DESERTS

The desert environment is harsh. Many people still like to visit. A trip to the desert can be risky. Even a short one can lead to disaster.

It was 2012. William LeFever was in Utah. He had to get to Page, Arizona. His father had sent him some money, and LeFever needed to pick it up.

Page was 90 miles away. LeFever didn't own a car. He decided to hike part of the way. Then he would get a ride. The trip should have taken a few days. Instead, the man got lost in Utah's Escalante Desert.

LeFever decided to follow a river. This kept him **hydrated**. He ate river frogs and **foraged** for plants. At night, small fires kept him warm. Rescuers struggled to find the missing man. A helicopter crew eventually spotted him sitting in shallow water. Over three weeks, this survivor had hiked 40 miles.

UTAH
ARIZONA

GPS can be helpful. Sometimes it makes mistakes though. One mistake almost cost Amber VanHecke her life. In 2017, she went to the Grand Canyon. The GPS took her down the wrong road. Soon the car ran out of gas. VanHecke was stranded. Right away, she **rationed** her food. On the second day, she made a sign. Rocks spelled out "HELP."

Four days passed. VanHecke thought about her family and tried to stay positive. The young woman felt she had more to do in life. The next day, VanHecke decided to move in search of phone service.

After walking 11 miles, VanHecke found cell service. She called 911 and returned to camp. A rescue helicopter came. The pilot saw her "HELP" sign. VanHecke said that thoughts of her family helped her survive.

Aron Ralston was a **mountaineer**. In 2003, he went for a day trip in Utah. Suddenly, the man fell down a small canyon. A large boulder fell on him. It weighed 800 pounds. His hand and arm were pinned.

Ralston did not panic. Instead, he thought of ways to get free. Nothing worked. The climber stayed positive. After three days, he began to get sick.

Two days later, Ralston worried he might die. He tried one last idea. The climber made a **tourniquet**. Then he took a small knife to his arm. More than an hour later, the arm was cut off. Finally free, Ralston had to climb down a cliff. After hiking for miles, the survivor was rescued. Ralston's story was made into a movie called *127 Hours*.

DEADLY DESERT CREATURES

North American deserts can be dangerous. Many deadly animals live there. The western diamondback is a rattlesnake. It is venomous. This means its bite can kill. People need emergency care right away. Coral snakes are venomous too. These reptiles are small, but their venom is strong. Without help, a bite can cause a heart attack.

The Mexican beaded lizard has venom too. So does the Gila monster. Both are found in Mexico. Gila monsters also live in the American Southwest. Their venom enters victims when the lizards chew on them.

Deserts are also home to many spiders. Black widow bites hurt. These can feel like bee stings. Some people have bad reactions. They cannot move parts of their body. Children can die. The Arizona brown spider is also dangerous. Bites can cause body tissue to die.

CHAPTER 5
MOUNTAINS

Mountains are wild places. Weather can be brutal. Storms bring strong winds, rain, and snow. There is often little food or shelter. In emergencies, climbers and hikers are often on their own.

Dylan Zitawi and Colton Lulfs were friends. In 2017, the pair went hiking in Washington State. A storm was coming. The two friends thought they could get through a mountain pass in time. They were wrong.

During the blizzard, snow piled up. It reached their chests. Zitawi and Lulfs made camp. In the morning, the storm raged on. The hikers were trapped. They turned on a rescue **beacon**. Help did not come.

Two days later, the snow stopped. Avalanche danger was high. Their food was running out. Finally they heard a helicopter. Rescuers had arrived just in time.

It was 2000. Tommy Caldwell and three friends were in Kyrgyzstan. All were professional rock climbers. Their adventure was risky from the start. There were armed rebels in the mountains. One day, the climbers woke to gunfire. The rebels took the group **hostage**. The men were given little food and water. They were forced to march in freezing cold weather.

After six days, the climbers were left with a guard. Caldwell made a hard decision. He pushed the guard off a cliff. The man lived. But this gave the climbers time to escape.

The group made it to a military outpost. They were rescued. Each person had lost about 20 pounds.

THE THIRD MAN FACTOR

In extreme situations, some people hear a voice. They see or feel a person nearby. This person gives advice. It helps them stay positive or guides them to safety. But no one is really there.

This experience is called the Third Man. The name comes from a poem. Many survivors have felt it. Some people believe it is a guardian angel. Many scientists think it is the brain triggering a survival response. Either way, the Third Man helps people survive.

CHAPTER 6
OUTER SPACE

In outer space, there is no oxygen. Radiation from the sun can be deadly. Few people have been to outer space. Some astronauts have had to fight to survive.

Luca Parmitano was an astronaut from Italy. In 2013, he was on the International Space Station (ISS). There was work to be done outside. Parmitano wore a spacesuit. Suddenly, he felt something wet on his neck. Parmitano tasted the liquid. It was coolant. This keeps spacesuits cool. Now it was leaking into his suit.

The astronaut rushed to the **airlock**. Parmitano had to flip around. A glob of liquid moved. His eyes and nose were covered. Breathing through his mouth, he tried to stay calm. Once inside, the astronaut had to wait. The airlock needed time to pressurize. Team members took off his helmet. Almost half a gallon of liquid had leaked. This astronaut was lucky to be alive.

LUCA PARMITANO
TEST PILOT
LUCA PARMITANO

In 2008, Peggy Whitson had command of the ISS. She was the first woman to be in charge. After six months, the astronaut was returning to Earth. Two other astronauts were with her. All three were in a **module**. During reentry, disaster struck.

Part of the module did not break off in the right way. This threw the craft off course. A fire started on the outside of the module. It began falling too fast. They fell 400,000 feet in 23 minutes. The crew struggled to breathe.

The module hit the ground. It landed 300 miles off course. Local people pulled the crew from the wreck. Doctors treated them at a hospital. Nine years later, Whitson became the first woman to command the ISS twice.

MARS MISSIONS

NASA wants to send humans to Mars one day. They would need special tools and buildings to survive there. Astronauts want to go to the red planet to work on these challenges.

Dust storms are common on Mars. Winds can be 60 miles per hour. The planet is also very cold. It is about –80 degrees Fahrenheit. There are also dangerous levels of radiation on the planet. Figuring out how to protect people there is a big challenge.

CHAPTER 7
PRISONERS OF WAR

In times of war, soldiers can be captured. These people become prisoners of war (POWs). Enemies hold them captive. POWs have many stories of extreme survival.

Louis Zamperini was a track and field athlete. He competed in the 1936 Olympics. World War II was from 1939 to 1945. Zamperini joined the Army Air Corps. One day, the soldier was in a plane. It went down over the ocean. Most of the crew died. For 47 days, the survivors floated in the ocean. They reached the shore but were captured by the Japanese.

Guards tortured Zamperini. They did not give him food. He was forced to work. His **will** was strong. After two years, the war ended. Zamperini was rescued. A 2014 movie told his story. It was called *Unbroken*.

LOUIS ZAMPERINI

The Vietnam War lasted from 1955 to 1975. John McCain served as a pilot in the 1960s. While flying, a missile hit his plane. McCain barely survived. Both arms and a leg were broken. After landing in a lake, he almost drowned. Enemies attacked and took him to prison. They refused to treat his wounds. Guards gave him beatings instead. Soldiers wanted information. He would not say anything.

McCain was moved to a prison camp. There, he was put in **solitary confinement**. For two years, the POW lived like that. Beatings happened several times a week.

The prisoner grew sick and lost weight. To stay positive, McCain thought about books. He wrote books and plays in his mind. After five years, McCain was released.

In 2003, a U.S. Army unit was in Iraq. It was part of a large convoy. GPS was not working, and the unit took a wrong turn. They were lost. Enemies began to fire on them. Some soldiers escaped, but several were killed.

Six Americans were taken prisoner. No one knew if they would be killed. Many were badly injured. The soldiers were moved many times. They were in cells by themselves and had little food. After three weeks, they were rescued by fellow soldiers.

AMERICAN PRISONERS OF WAR

There have been many POWs from the United States. The country first went to war in 1775. This was the Revolutionary War. About 20,000 Americans were taken prisoner. A little more than half survived.

During World War II, many Americans were POWs. In Europe, 94,000 were captured. Almost 30,000 more were taken prisoner in the Pacific. Very few survived.

The Gulf War started in 1991. In Iraq, 23 Americans were captured. Many were beaten.

During the Iraq War, there were 10 American POWs. All were safely returned to the United States.

AMERICAN CAPTURED BY THE JAPANESE IN WWII

CHAPTER 8

CAVES

A cave can provide protection. It can be a shelter. Caves can also be deadly mazes. Luck is needed to survive.

In 2008, teens Alec Corbett and Alessandro Gelmini were exploring. They were in an ice cave in Washington. Suddenly, there was a loud crack. Blocks of ice fell. In an instant, the pair was trapped.

Corbett was pinned down under the ice. His face was pushed into a stream. Once the ice settled, the stream stopped. He could breathe again. Badly injured, the teens stayed calm. They took strength from each other. Friends and family feared the worst. That evening, search and rescue workers found them. Both had broken backs and ankles. Gelmini had injuries to his face and arm too. The pair was thankful to be alive.

Lukas Cavar was a college student. There was a caving club at his school. In 2017, the club went to a cave. They came to a difficult section. It was called the Backbreaker. Visitors have to hunch down. Cavar did not like that part. He hurried ahead and took a wrong turn.

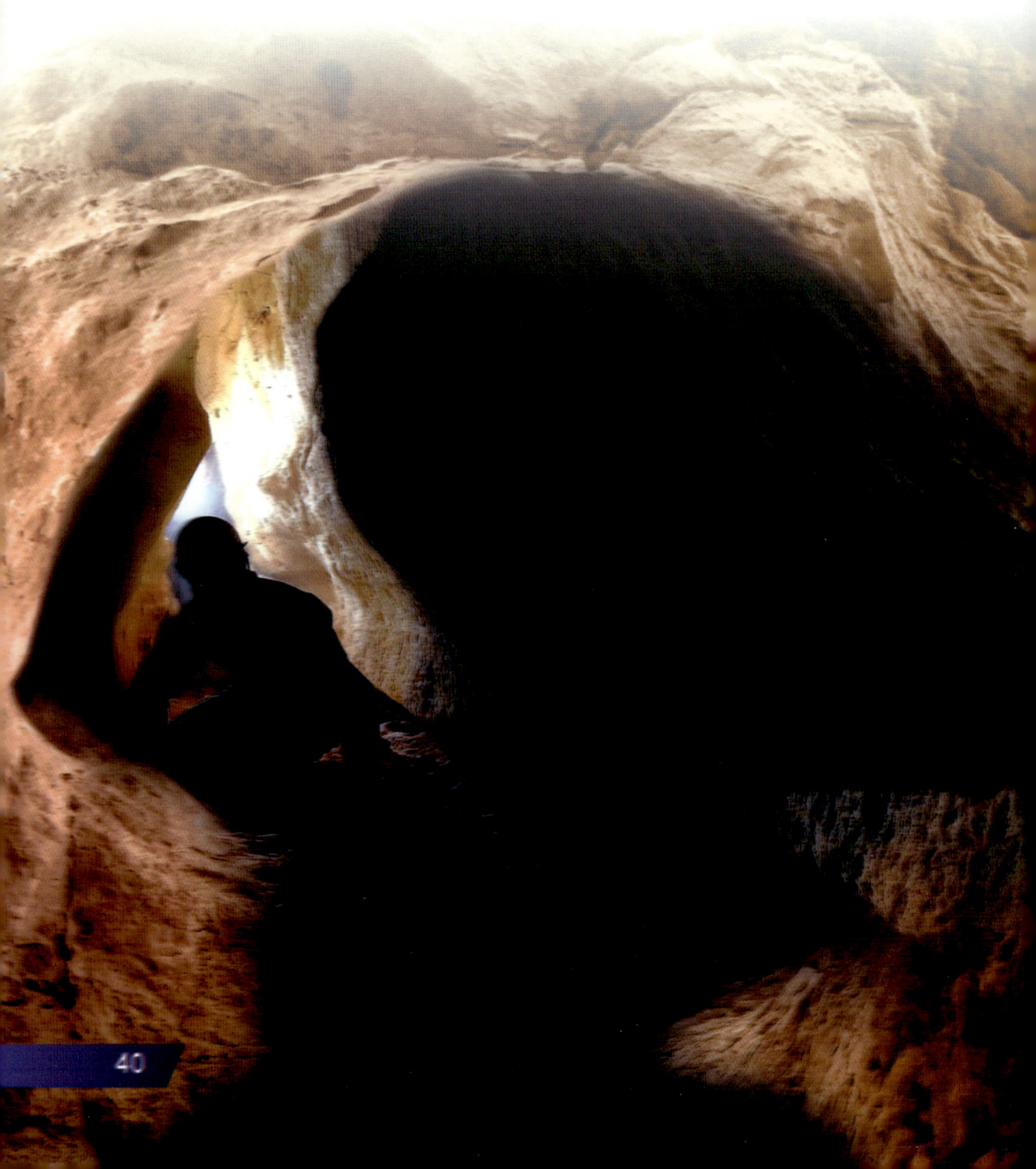

Realizing he was lost, the student stopped. Cavar waited. No one came. After several hours of searching, he found the exit. The gate was locked. With a paperclip, the caver tried to pick the lock. Hours went by.

Starting to panic, Cavar thought of his friends and family. This calmed him down. When it got cold, he walked around. For water, the student licked damp walls. Days went by. Hungry and weak, the survivor saw a flashlight. Rescue had come.

In 2018, Spencer and Jessica Christiansen took a trip. It was to ice caves in Wyoming. The couple planned a four-hour hike. Nine hours later, they were very lost. Temperatures were freezing.

On the second day, Jessica fell 20 feet. Spencer was able to catch her. By this time, they were wet. Hypothermia was a danger. Both had frostbite on their hands. They burned gear for warmth. Soon the food was all gone. After two days, the pair heard something. People were calling their names. The couple saw a flashlight. Rescuers found them. It was Spencer's birthday.

CAVE DIVING

Many caves are underwater. Using SCUBA gear, people can go diving in these areas. Cave diving is a popular sport, but it is also very dangerous.

Cave divers see beautiful sights. There are unique animals and plant life. Divers often have to swim through small passages. Sometimes they get lost. When this happens, it can mean trouble. Their oxygen might run out.

Many cave divers follow the rule of thirds. One third of their oxygen is for the way in. Another third is for the way out. The final third is saved. It is only used in emergencies.

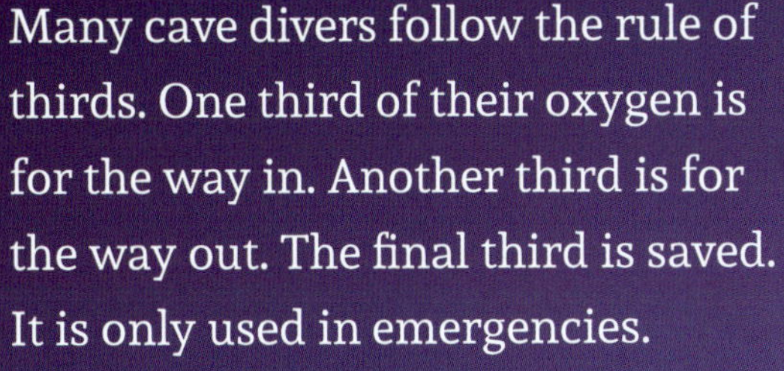

CHAPTER 9
NATURAL DISASTERS

Natural disasters strike every year. Each can claim lives. They can also create dangerous situations. People are forced to figure out a way to survive.

California was hot and dry in 2018. Large wildfires started. One was called the Camp Fire. It started early in the morning. Winds were blowing at 50 miles per hour. The fire grew quickly.

Brandon Hill was taking his kids to school. He saw the fire moving fast. Racing home, Hill picked up his wife and son. The family sped to Hill's mother's house in a nearby town.

Neighbors came to Hill's mother's house. Small fires popped up around the property. Everyone fought the fire. Some used garden hoses. Others used a tractor to dig a path the fire couldn't cross. A man came to the house, soaking wet. He needed help. People were trapped in a **reservoir**. Hill's son was 14. The boy took a canoe with some other people. They rescued the survivors. More than 85 people were killed by the Camp Fire. All of the Hill family survived.

It was 2017. Annie and Greg Smith were going to have a baby. Hurricane Harvey hit. Over the next few days, floodwaters rose. The hospital was only two miles away. But it was impossible for them to drive there. Annie went into labor.

A rescue crew arrived. Everyone linked arms. This formed a human chain through the deep water. Walking slowly along the chain, Annie held onto each person. She reached the truck. It took her to the hospital. Staff had been stuck there for days. After 12 more hours, the baby was born. Her nickname was "Little Harvey."

It was 2004. Peter Heydemann was in Thailand on vacation. One morning, the tide began to rise. Heydemann thought it was a high tide. He went to look. Suddenly, the man was underwater. A **tsunami** had hit.

Rushing water carried Heydemann inside a building. His body hit **debris**, which broke his arm. He was drowning when the building broke apart. The water was as high as the treetops. Heydemann grabbed a tree branch. It broke and the waters swept him to sea.

Clinging to a bodyboard, Heydemann floated. Using his good arm, he waved for help. No one saw him. The survivor made his way to the beach. People took him to a hospital. His family was reunited.

COSTLY U.S. NATURAL DISASTERS

Natural disasters destroy homes and buildings. Rebuilding and caring for survivors can cost billions.

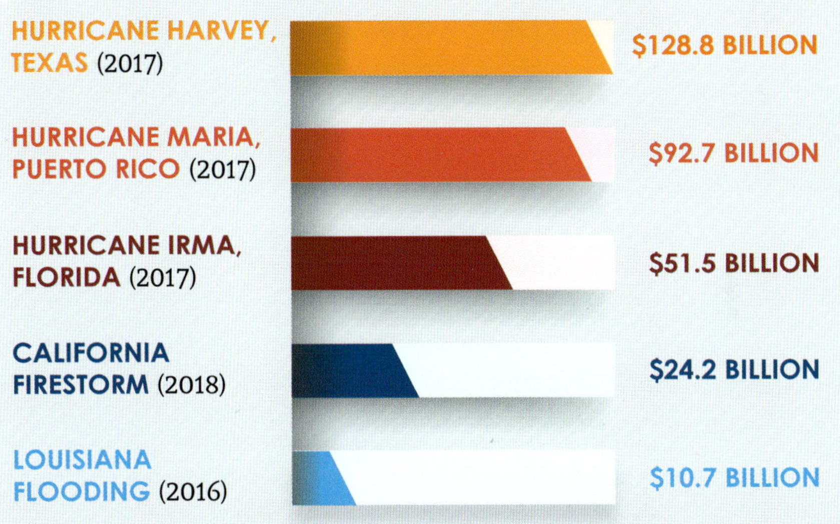

FIRE SHELTERS

Wildland firefighters work to put out fires like the Camp Fire. Each wildland firefighter carries a fire shelter. It is a thin piece of silver material. Firefighters lie facedown on the ground. They pull the shelter over them. The thin blanket traps air to allow them to breathe. Heat is reflected.

Using a fire shelter can be terrifying. But hundreds of lives have been saved.

CHAPTER 10
YOUNG SURVIVORS

Anyone can survive extreme events. Age does not matter. Many young people have made it through deadly situations alive.

Nicholas Joy enjoyed TV shows about survival. In 2013, Joy was 17. While skiing, he got lost. Rescuers were searching for the young man. The weather was stormy. They could not find him.

The teen used tips from the shows to save his life. At night, it was very cold. Temperatures were about 20 degrees Fahrenheit. Joy built a shelter. It was made from branches and snow. He drank water from streams.

During the day, Joy walked toward the sounds of snowmobiles. He found tracks and followed them to safety. Two days had passed. Joy had **hypothermia**. The teen was lucky to be alive.

THE NORTH FACE
NICHOLAS JOY

In 2005, Jaimie Cummings was 14. She was with her mother in a New Orleans hospital. Cummings heard a storm. The rain and wind were loud. It was Hurricane Katrina.

SURVIVAL GEAR

People should carry certain gear while on potentially risky adventures, including water, food, and shelter. Then they can survive in extreme situations.

A bottle is needed to carry water while on the go. In an emergency, water can be collected from streams. It needs to be purified to kill harmful bacteria. There are tablets that can purify water. A small water filter can also be used.

For food, experts say to carry energy bars. They are high in protein. This nutrient keeps muscles strong. Bars also have a lot of fat that helps power the body.

An emergency blanket should be carried. It keeps the body warm at night. These blankets do not breathe well. They can trap moisture. During the day, turn it inside out so it can dry.

A compass or GPS is also important. These help adventurers stay on track or find their way when they get lost.

When the power went out, people started to panic. They had to get out. Cummings and her mom walked through deep floodwaters. Dead bodies floated by. It took hours to reach the exit.

Police put Cummings and her mother on a boat. A helicopter took them to Texas. Their neighborhood had been destroyed. They never moved back.

It was 2015. Autumn Veatch was 16. She was traveling from Montana to Washington with her step-grandparents. Both of them were pilots and were flying a small plane. Suddenly, they started to fall. The plane hit trees. Then it hit the ground and caught on fire. Veatch was the only survivor.

Veatch fell off a small cliff. She kept going. That night, it was freezing cold. The woods were very thick. Eventually, the teen found a road. No cars came.

The young woman reached a parking lot. Unable to stand, she sat down. That's when two people found her. The teen had burns and cuts and was dehydrated. But she survived. A local sheriff said Veatch was a determined and strong lady.

Reading extreme survival stories can be thrilling. They describe deadly situations and the people who survive them. No one wants to be in an emergency event. It takes strength and determination to stay alive. These tales can help inspire people who find themselves in unexpected situations.

a room on a spaceship with two entrances that can be sealed tightly to allow no air to leave

BEACON
a bright light or radio signal used to call for help

BIOLOGIST
a scientist that works with living things like plants and animals

COAST GUARD
an organization that guards the waters just off of a country's land; provides help for people in trouble at sea

DEBRIS
broken pieces left after something is destroyed

FORAGE
to search for food

GORE
to stab with a horn or tusk

HOSTAGE
a person captured by another person who wants something in return

HYDRATED
having enough water

HYPOTHERMIA
a condition in which a person's body temperature is too low

MODULE
part of a spacecraft that can be flown or driven on its own

MOUNTAINEER
a person who is skilled at mountain climbing

RATION
to preserve a set amount of something to use over a certain period of time

RESERVOIR
a large lake used as a water supply

RESOURCEFULNESS
the ability to deal with difficult situations and solve problems

SOLITARY CONFINEMENT
being kept alone in a cell for punishment

THREATENING
able to cause harm or injury

TOURNIQUET
a device used to apply pressure to a limb to stop blood loss; can also be used to stop the spread of poison through the body

TSUNAMI
a very large wave in the ocean that is usually caused by an earthquake

WILL
a strong determination to do something

INCREDIBLE COMEBACKS

HURRICANE STRENGTH

In each baseball game, almost 150 pitches are thrown. Pitchers tend to have injuries, often from overuse of certain muscles.

Pitches average 92 miles per hour. That is the speed of hurricane winds. Pitchers want to throw fast. Speed makes balls harder to hit. Over the years, pitchers have learned to throw faster. But this is harder on their bodies. Muscle strains and tears happen more often.

WORLD SERIES DROUGHTS

Baseball teams often go through droughts. In sports, a drought is a period of time a team goes without reaching a goal, like making it to a championship game. Many teams have had long World Series droughts. But some droughts end in comebacks. The following graph shows how long it took some MLB teams to overcome their droughts.

Sue Bird is in the WNBA. She plays point guard. From 2007 to 2013, the player had a rough time. During those years, Bird had multiple injuries. The athlete had surgeries on her knee and hip. A broken nose needed surgery too. Each operation meant months of healing time. In 2013, the sportswoman did not play. Every day, she worked on recovering.

Then Bird came back better than ever. She played in All-Star games. These were in 2014 and 2015. At the 2016 Olympic Games, the athlete won gold. Her game stayed strong. Bird was an All-Star in 2017 and 2018 too.

CHAPTER 5
FOOTBALL

Football is a full-contact sport. This means players tackle each other. Athletes have to be tough.

J.J. Watt is a Houston Texans star. He was in the Pro Bowl every year from 2012 to 2015. Then the athlete needed back surgery. The defensive end missed most games in 2016. Watt spent his time in recovery.

FOR MORE TITLES AND INFORMATION →

space ∞

9781680217513

9781680217575

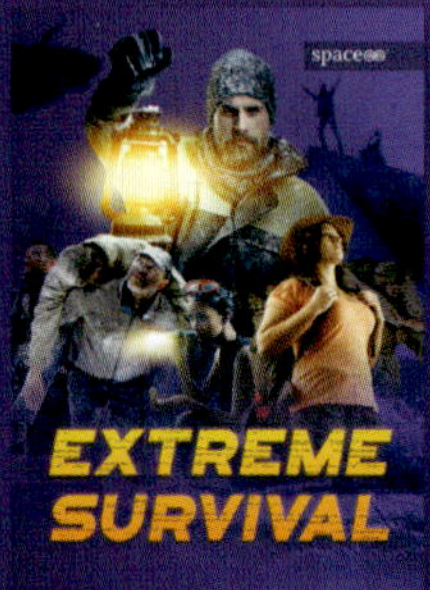

9781680217483

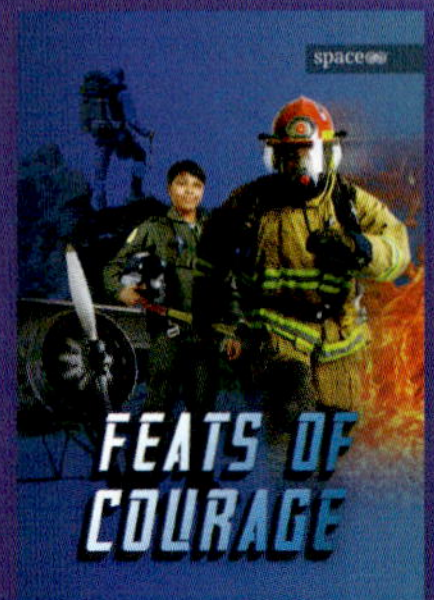

9781680217476

9781680217469

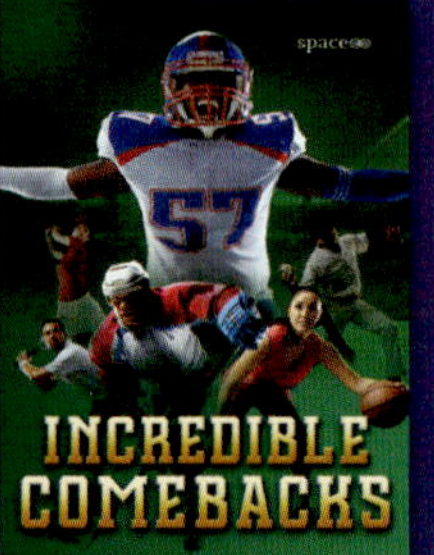

9781680217490

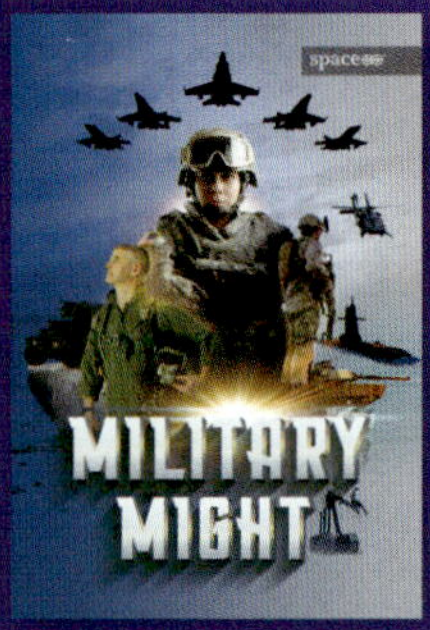

9781680217520

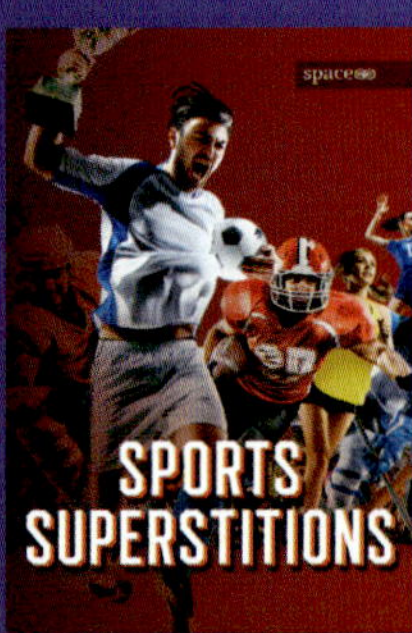

9781680217445

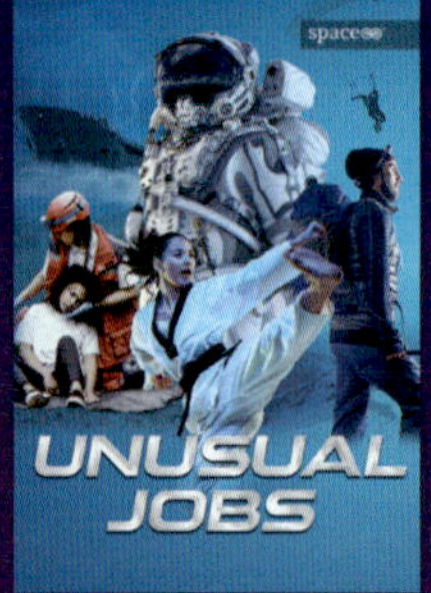

9781680217568

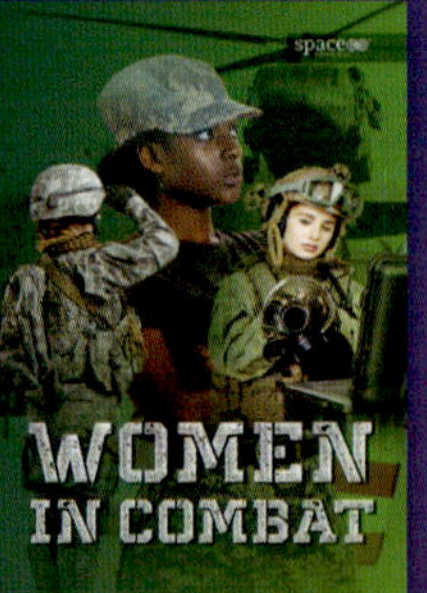

9781680217506

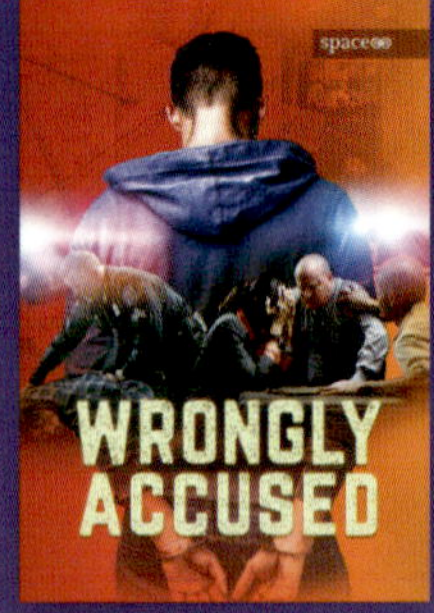

9781680217452

MORE TITLES COMING SOON

sdlback.com/Space-8